Home Visiting Those at Risk of Addiction, Antisocial and Offending Behaviour - A Practice Study Guide

Pastoral Care in Criminal and Social Justice Series

www.metanoeo.weebly.com

If you would like Metanoeo to deliver the contents of this study guide as a training workshop for your organisation then please use the contact form at:

www.metanoeo.weebly.com

Introduction

Have you ever visited a client and on your way wondered, 'why am I going today'? If so, then you're not alone, the research that underpins this workbook suggests this is a common question for many criminal justice practitioners; am I checking up on them, am I visiting to show I care, am I visiting to see who they are living with and what their home is like?

With this variety of perspectives on offer the author undertook a piece of research with probation staff and service users to discover what perspectives they held on home visiting and how this could be used to undertake more effective and purposeful home visits.

From its institutional Christian missionary roots the Probation Service has been a continually evolving organisation (Nellis, 1998). Departing from the initial aim of 'advising, assisting and befriending' the offender, practitioners now operate in a climate of increased focus on risk assessment and public protection (Buchanan and Millar, 1997). This has impacted upon practice as the Probation Service has sought to present a tougher public image (Millar and Buchanan, 1995). This is a backdrop which will be familiar to many criminal justice professionals and those working in the sector of addiction, antisocial and offending behaviour. Many practitioners are motivated by their care for people, but find themselves operating in a risk focused context. This implies home visiting requires a careful balancing of priorities for practitioners. Hence, this workbook aims to help practitioners consider how they can best achieve effective home visits considering the potential for their use.

The Structure of this Workbook

This workbook aims to provoke discussion on this topic through presenting a literature review on home visiting and the findings of a piece of research undertaken by the author examining client's views on home visits. It concludes challenging the reader to consider for themselves what role home visiting can play in developing their own practice. Throughout the workbook there are question breaks where you are encouraged to pause and reflect on the material you have just read and how it might be applied to your own practice within your own context. Indeed, it is time for the first one now …

Question Break 1

Consider what your initial thoughts are on the purpose of home visiting in your own practice.

Chapter 1 - Thinking about the lessons of history

In thinking about practice with those at risk of addiction, antisocial and offending behaviour this workbook will consider the development of the work of the probation service as providing an easily identifiable history in this area. Whilst it is outside the realm of this workbook to examine the development of the modern Probation Service, the changing context of practice concerning the use of home visiting can be understood in its relevance to the service's historical development. For the early Police Court Missionary home visiting formed a crucial part of how the work was undertaken with visits not only being made to see the offender, but also to speak to family members, employers, educators and other important people in the individual's life (Mair, 1997). Direct visits would be made to women working the streets as prostitutes with the aim of assisting them to secure accommodation and help them secure employment. Home visiting was an essential part of the community basis to the work undertaken, with the recorded work being completed in the usual environment of the offender.

As time progressed the Service was placed on a formal statutory basis and the early theological influences on practice begun to be replaced, at least from an organisational perspective. This led to the ministerial approach to practice no longer being the primary driving factor to the structure of the work undertaken with offenders. As the theory developed through the emerging social sciences was engaged home visiting once again became an important means of practice albeit now from a social work as opposed to a ministerial perspective. Buchanan and Millar (1997) describe the characteristics of this 'social work practice' as effectively engaging with clients which would require an appreciation of their personal circumstances, clearly placing the focus of the supervision in the community through highlighting the need for practitioners to understand the social context of their clients.

Over the past few decades, as the changes have continued, the political, academic and social context has been set for major criticism and changes to the traditional values held by the Probation Service. Discussion would now take place around the value for money presented by interventions. Social need would have to take a second place to an emphasis on economy, efficiency and effectiveness (Senior, 1987). Managers of the Probation Service recognised that it must depart from being a 'welfare' organisation to concentrate its resources on those who posed the biggest risk of reoffending (Boswell and Worthington, 1991). With a lack of political agreement for the Service's traditional values, it needed to redefine itself as an organisation that was efficient and had a specific purpose in the criminal justice system. The Probation Service would now exist to divert individuals from custody (Rex, 1999). Further, throughout recent times, public and politicians have been jointly presented as expecting criminal justice to be singularly focused on reducing crime (Hudson, 2001) and not a 'soft' approach of offender welfare. The introduction of National Standards had been, at least in part, aimed at addressing these issues through reassuring sentencers and the public that community-based Order's were not a 'soft option' and that failure to co-operate with supervision would be taken seriously (Hedderman and Hearnden, 2001). In terms of the impact this would have on home visiting, whilst policies and practice standards continue to require home visits medium, high and very high risk of harm cases within ten working days of sentence / release from prison on licence (Home Office, 2005) the purpose of these visits were no longer as self-evident as they may once have been to the ministerial minded or social work trained practitioner. Home visits formed only a negligible required part of a more prescribed set standard for supervision. Compounding this was also the lack of discussion on the use of home visiting from the Ministry of Justice and the National Offender Management Service. Indeed, when searching for guidance on home visiting practice the only contemporary documents discovered where local practice requirements on the risk assessment of home visits. The contemporary question posed for practitioners has therefore become, 'what difference will home visiting make to risk management and effective supervision?'

Question Break 2

What is the fundamental expectation of home visits from the context your organisation works in?

Chapter 2 - The use of visiting in other services - A home visits literature review

In examining the context of Probation practice it is undeniable that there has been a great many theoretical influences and motivations on the basis of practice as hinted at above. Acknowledging this paves the way to examining what can be gleaned through understanding how home visits are used in these associated professions and services as the theory and thinking influencing these services will have been echoed in Probation practice during its history and hence will still have a bearing through the ongoing development of practice on current methods. Further to this, there is a crossover between the type of work undertaken between these other services and professions and the work undertaken by the criminal and community justice practitioner's service working with people at risk of addiction, antisocial and offending behaviour.

Pastoral Visiting

Beginning with pastoral visiting in the ecclesiastical setting; the pastoral minister needs the respect of their parishioners in order to undertake their ministry, a sentiment which is also relevant to the criminal justice practitioner seeking to be successful in their work. Griffith-Thomas (1995) in his book on the work of the minister notes how home visiting can influence a ministers understanding of their congregation and the congregations' respect for their minister. Continuing with the pastoral, Hockling (1985) highlights a number of functions; demonstrating an interest in individuals, getting to know people and their background, and being available to help and advise them. These aspects of home visiting are crucial to developing the authority required to carry out any further ministry as it is recognised that authority by office carries no real meaning without relationship (Carr, 2002) and thus the visit is a tool in developing the relationship. Clearly, all these aspects could similarly be used in contemporary criminal justice practice and traditionally have formed part of the purpose of home visits.

Capps (1982) highlights how visits can be used to undertake a less formal type of counselling, 'pastoral conversation'. This is linked to Wright's (1982) observation that the visitor's physical presence in the home can be the most important factor, essentially as the visitor can act as a sustainer through their presence as opposed to their actions or words whilst there. This principle can be extended in so much as a visitor can also increase their profile with the individual's family (Hornsby-Smith, 1989), an important factor in working with individuals who are only likely to have limited contact with a professional offering an intervention whilst spending the rest of the time with their family. This should reassure the criminal justice practitioner that in undertaking a visit, it is often their presence in the home, showing interest to the individual and their family, which can mean more than the work they attempt to undertake whilst there. However, this link with the family is an important point as additionally an increased profile with the family will also give an increased informal knowledge of the individual as family behaviour patterns and beliefs can be observed (Ross, 2003). A final organisational point to home visiting is made by Wright (1996) who observes that visiting makes for an outward looking church. In the case of your organisation, this could serve to help base you in the community as an 'outward' community-focused organisation as opposed to one that could run the risk otherwise of becoming focused on its own sustenance (which is a sentiment often felt by a numbers of practitioners in relation to meeting targets and completing numerous pro-forma).

Question Break 3

What aspects of pastoral / ministerial visiting might be relevant to your undertaking of home visits?

Medical Professions

Within the medical professions it appears evident that home visiting can and is used to reduce health risks through the provision of a more supportive service to patients (Ciliska, et al, 2001). Home visits are also seen to be a way in the medical professions of gathering information on; family structure (McMurray, 1990) and history (Crosbie, et al, 1994); locally available community services that would be of use to the patient (D'Angelo, 1999); and what is required in terms of support for a patient (O'Connor and Gibson, 2003). Clearly all these factors would also be relevant to the criminal justice professional where it is vital for a worker with limited time to attempt to link an individual into services within their community and to understand their personal circumstances. In addition to the above, Robertson (1991) notes how home visits can be utilised in treating patients whose low self-esteem would prevent them engaging in treatment in another setting and also highlights how visits can help the practitioner concentrate on the role of the whole family in the provision of the treatment. Linking this to criminal justice interventions, this could offer individuals who struggle to engage in the office the opportunity to be worked with where they feel more comfortable and with the support of their family. A final point of note comes from McNaughton (2000) who reviewed fourteen pieces of research and concluded where home visiting programmes were based upon a good client-professional relationship the visit could be an empowering experience giving the client some power back in the relationship with the professional as they were guests in their home.

Question Break 4

What aspects of medical visiting might be relevant to your undertaking of home visits?

Social Work Practice

In relation to home visiting in social work practice, Azar and Ferraro (2000) argue that whilst an office visit may allow freedom from the distractions provided in a family home, these very distractions allow a contextualisation of the individual through seeing the natural family behaviour. Further, they believe there is greater potential for generalised application of any work being undertaken as it is occurring in the natural habitat of the learner who can instantly relate lessons to their everyday experiences. Visits are also seen as a useful method of giving the visited someone to relate to personally and relay their concerns to in the non-formal setting of their home (Frankel and Hobart, 1998). These principles have been utilised in the Home-Start initiative where the home visiting component of the programme is planned to provide parents with long-term friendship, support and practical help (Hopkins, 2003).

Home visiting is seen to form an important part of any social work assessment of a child who may be at risk as usual family and neighbourhood interactions can be witnessed firsthand by the professional (Vaughn, 1984) giving a direct opportunity to assess any risk related to these areas. Clearly, once again, these principles can be easily extended to cover the informing of the justice practitioners assessment of risk in a given case. However, it is not just the assessment that is impacted by home visiting. Sturkie (1984) notes that home visits, "may be used to help engage a family by making members feel less stigmatised and threatened ..." (p.78). Barlow et al (2003) build on this arguing that structured home visiting programmes can be used to promote positive parenting techniques and hence be used to offer positive alternatives in behaviour for the visited. Gardner (2005) also reports that home visiting schemes are used as a protective factor in preventing crisis through offering friendship and practical support. Hence, the visit in addition to informing assessment can also form part of the action plan necessitated by that assessment.

 Question Break 5

What aspects of social work visiting might be relevant to your undertaking of home visits?

Other Criminal Justice Partners

Finally, looking at the impact of criminal justice organisations' home visits, whilst there was not much contemporary writing on home visits in Probation practice there was nevertheless some positive information available. In the United Kingdom, the Home Office (2006) discovered that a partnership project between Probation, the Police and a drug rehabilitation agency found that regular home visiting served to bolster offender's commitment to remain drug and offence free, although it was unclear as to whether this was due to the perceived support or surveillance that the home visits could have provided. Further encouragement could also be taken that home visiting was still seen a "staple component" of supervision in New York, USA (New York City Department of Probation, 2006) where visits were used to assess how an individual is progressing in their home and community.

Question Break 6

What aspects of visiting in this chapter have struck you as relevant to your undertaking of home visits?

Chapter 3 - Discovering the thoughts of those being visited

With the historical background of the Probation Service and literature review considered, the views of current service users are also important to understand in order to ensure the work completed is targeted effectively. For example, undertaking pastorally motivated visits would be of little use if the majority of clients felt home visits were purposed toward 'checking up'. A part-quantitative, part-qualitative questionnaire was developed to this end and used with a sample of twenty-one practitioners and fifty-one clients determined through random nomination by members of staff and then through agreement to participate by the client. The aim of this method of sampling was to identify participants who would be willing to engage with the research and offer their opinions in confidence. Whilst it should be acknowledged that this method may have risked attracting clients with a more positive attitude to the service, in practice many offered both positive and negative comments both in relation to their views on home visiting and the quality of supervision they had received from the service. It would therefore appear that the confidentiality and anonymity offered may have encouraged an open dialogue. With regards to the profile of the sample the vast majority of clients in the geographical area are white British and this was reflected in the survey population with only two from non-white ethnic groups. Given the nature of the research was to provoke discussion and consideration on potential uses of home visits as opposed to giving a didactic methodology to visiting this may not prove that important in relation to the usefulness and applicability of the findings. Nevertheless, the low ethnic variation in those surveyed did limit the opportunity to research diversity issues in relation to visiting with cultural respectfulness.

The quantitative element of the questionnaire asked questions relating to aspects of home visiting and whether the participating (a) felt they reflected the purpose of visits and (b) were important to home visits. This was split into three main themes; understanding and knowledge of the client and their background, knowing and engaging the family (or whoever the client usually resided with), and practitioner-service user relationships / practice related questions. The qualitative section sought clarification of the quantitative data and also questioned whether more visits should be made and what would improve the quality of home visits.

Question Break 7

What implications might the methodology and sample have on applying the findings to your context?

Findings from the Primary Research

We will now look at the findings of the research, and in particular, how the clients viewed home visiting. Given your own context may be different to that of the probation practitioner, practitioners views have only been included where they may help to make sense of the service user's perspective.

Understanding and Knowledge

The first stream of questions demonstrated service users felt home visits were fairly to very important as a means of helping practitioners understand the individual, their home life and their individual needs. The particular area that was felt as being of most importance to home visiting was that of helping practitioner to understand any risks posed. For practitioners this might have been considered their primary purpose in home visiting, recognising that more consistent home visiting could improve their risk assessment through better and more regular contact with other family members and increased contextual understanding of their clients. A further point in the understanding and knowledge stream of questions related to the undeveloped potential of exploiting existing local services; that is practitioners using their visits to discover local services in the client's locality which they could link them into. Whilst service users were far more positive in their understanding of practitioners visiting them to help know what services were available to them in their locality, practitioners recognised that whilst this was currently rarely a purpose of their visits, this could form an important part of the reason they undertook home visits in the future.

Question Break 8

What implications might the methodology and sample have on applying the findings to your context?

Engaging Family Members

The second series of questions related to the practitioners engagement with family members during home visits. Attitudes were measured toward home visits being used to meet client's families, helping their family understand the role of the service offered, engaging them with the goals of the service and offering the family help and support. Of all the questions asked, this stream scored the lowest although there was a significant difference of opinion between practitioners and clients relating to the use of home visits to involve the family. Whilst clients felt this was not that important a reason to make home visits, most believed this was a significant motivation for practitioners in undertaking visits. Practitioners however felt that whilst they did not really visit for that purpose, it could become a fairly important purpose for visiting. Overall, whilst some practitioners and service users felt involving other members of the family could interfere with the confidentiality of the service, there was a general agreement that meeting the family could help understand the individual and that in some cases involving the family could be helpful in complementing the service's work through the more constant and long-term support available from family members.

Question Break 9

How could you make better use of the friends and families of your clients through home visiting and what concerns might this raise?

Developing the Working Relationship

Examining the third stream of questions it was evident that it was in the development of the working relationship that service users and practitioners agreed home visiting was both most important and the most significant motivation for undertaking visits. There was a clear emphasis that all felt home visiting evidenced valuing relationships and demonstrated a commitment to those visited. However, there was a warning to be heeded in this respect as whilst the working relationship could be strengthened through home visits, one service user noted that it could also be weakened if they were to feel their home was being visited and not them; a reference to visiting as purely a means of collating information. With regards to practice development, although there was some indication that practitioners and service users recognised the home could provide a real life context for developing new skills and behaviours, there was hesitation to using the home as a 'contextualised classroom'.

Question Break 10

How aware are you of the impact of your home visits on your relationship with your client and how could you use this better?

Quantity of Visits

In relation to the quantity of home visits made 86% of practitioners questioned felt the number of visits made should be increased in comparison to 49% of service users. However, this result is not as straightforward as it may at first appear. When explanation was sought for the response to this question the overwhelming theme was that the quantity and frequency of home visits should be judged on a case-by-case basis. When qualifying their answer with this statement, there was a much more positive view expressed to increased home visiting by service users (although a second measurement quantifying this was not taken). Given this information, there is an important warning here in that increased home visiting should not be formalised through a set standard requirement but should be responsive to the individual client. Perhaps there is a danger given the current economic agenda of strong quantitative classification of work for 'efficiency, economy and accountability' that an increased focus on home visiting could miss the point by setting visiting targets across the board which lack in the individual responsivity that is necessary when deciding when and how many visits should be made.

Question Break 11

How could you assess the frequency and quantity of home visiting required for each of your cases?

Thinking About the Quality of Visits

Concerning improving the quality of the visits experienced a significant lesson is the feeling that visits should be made for a clear purpose, honestly explained. Further learning points related to using the home visit as an 'emblem of joint enterprise' through recognising that the practitioner was entering the clients home and thus respecting their privacy as far as possible and also visiting at a mutually convenient time. This is important as there is a danger that visits could be perceived as an unwarranted invasion of the privacy of the individual's home. The main concerns voiced by practitioners as to their experience of home visits firstly related to undertaking visits when experiencing high workloads and secondly to the potential risks posed to themselves in home visiting. In relation to the latter, whilst there was little indication from records of staff facing violence when undertaking home visits, completing a sensible and proper risk assessment prior to home visiting is essential. Dealing with the former, practitioners did voice genuine concerns over the time taken up in completing home visits. The only practical response that can realistically be made in relation to these concerns is that targeted home visiting with a focused purpose may make for more effective and thus efficient use of time as opposed to home visits with no real aim just because a policy requires the visit. This is therefore once again a warning that simply imposing a home visiting policy across the board with a lack of flexibility is unlikely to make for effective practice and indeed would most probably result in increased pressure for practitioners potentially leading to a lack of quality work.

Question Break 12

How can you best plan and risk assess a safe and purposeful home visit?

Chapter 4 - Considering the findings in the light of the current research context

There has been much writing over recent years on refocusing practice on the centrality of the client-service user relationship to promoting desistance from crime. This research suggests both practitioners and clients believe home visiting can form part of the development this relationship. Davies (2006) suggests that committed attention from practitioners in developing the working relationship was more important than the methodology employed in motivating and engaging clients. Similarly, McNeill (2004) found the individual approach of personal relationships to be more important than the generalised approach of programmes or interventions on their own. McNeill (2006) also writes that, "desistance-supporting interventions ... need to be based on legitimate and respectful relationships ..." (p55). In this research, clients clearly felt home visits enabled trust, a better working relationship and demonstrated an interest being shown in them which would help achieve Davies' and McNeill's points. McCulloch and Kelly (2007) also argue that there is a 'who works' incentive in that the effectiveness of work is underpinned by clients perceptions of practitioners. Again, the personal interest and time taking in undertaken a home visit can encourage the development of the working relationship required to achieve this status of respect with the client. The essential message here is that the practitioner-service user relationship is still viewed as an important tool for effective practice (Bracken, 2003) and home visiting is a tool which can promote the development of that relationship and the 'who works' agenda.

Question Break 13

How could you use home visits to develop a 'who works' agenda?

Well planned visiting can also give practitioners the opportunity to engage with and advocate for their client's needs within their social context and network which Burnett and McNeil (2005) have suggested are significant in the promotion of desistance. Indeed, part of the National Offender Management Service' Offender Management Model suggests using community resources with clients should become part of 'core correctional practice' (National Offender Management Service, 2006). As discussed above, there is potential for the development of this brokerage and advocacy through using home visiting to strengthen ties with services in their local community.

Question Break 14

How can you better plan your home visits to advocate for your clients and link them to local community based services?

Nevertheless, there was a warning provided in the primary research here that the use of home visits that are not perceived to be for genuine interest in and benefit for the client but just to assess their lifestyle could negatively impact on the working relationship. This does highlight the importance of balancing the additional information that can be gathered through visiting to inform risk assessment, such as seeing interpersonal family relationships, with the importance of visits being perceived as a relationship making tool. In some cases, the comments made by those visited who were interviewed would suggest they are likely to be wary of what the motivation may be for staff in undertaking their visit believing practitioners may be 'checking up' on them. However, for others, the home visit is a genuine means of showing interest and giving quality time. Again this highlights the individual approach that must be utilised in effectively undertaking home visits. These concerns may be reinforced by the current political agenda in which talk about rehabilitation tends to be focused on 'getting them to go straight' as opposed to restoration to the status as a full member of the local community (Merrington, 2006) and thus simply becomes a tool for crime reduction (Lewis, 2005). Where staff practice home visits with this in mind, there is always the danger that the benefits discussed above of showing a genuine interest in the offender will not be achievable as the motivation for the visit may be perceived as alternative and ingenuous, undertaking the visit to help achieve their own aims or to add to the government surveillance of and desire to impose change on their life.

Question Break 15

What issues are pertinent to your practice context which will impact on how your visits are perceived and what can you do about these?

Conclusion

It was evident in this research that for many the only contemporary discussion around home visiting was related to undertaking visits to meet policies and processes. Despite the recent plethora of policy documents produced at a national and local level relating to working with those at risk of addiction, antisocial and offending behaviour, this oversight has not been rectified. This workbook attempts to reignite this discussion through demonstrating that far from being a historical legacy of practice from a bygone era do-gooders, those at risk of addiction, antisocial and offending behaviour still view home visits as an important part of the work undertaken with them. Further, home visiting can be used as an integral part of contemporary practice to improve the quality of assessment and the effectiveness of the intervention offered through an improved client-practitioner relationship.

Although the primary research here was only a small study, the literary research demonstrated home visiting continues to be an effective means of practice in many disciplines and appeared to confirm the positive indications from the research. Home visiting is certainly not a practice that can be applied in a systematic and prescribed manner in order to be effective, for example, Brorson (2005) warns of the importance of adjusting to each homes 'cultural environment' which is in addition to considering the individual demands and needs of each individual visited. Indeed, there may be some clients for which home visits are not helpful, and some staff for which it is not practical. The challenge to the modern practitioner working in the field of addiction, antisocial and offending behaviour would thus appear to be to consider for themselves how they utilise home visiting in their own practice given the individual case-by-case application that is required. Without such a contemporary debate and consideration there is a very real danger that home visiting could otherwise become a forgotten art of intervention relegated to a task undertaken in a systemised manner to fulfil policies and procedures.

Question Break 16

What are the three main learning points from this workbook which you will apply to your practice?

References

Azar, S and Ferraro, M (2000), 'How Can Parenting be Enhanced?' in Dubowitz, H and DePanfilis, D (ed's), *Handbook for Child Protection Practice,* London: Sage Publications Inc

Barlow, J, Stewart-Brown, S, Callaghan, H, Tucker, J, Brocklehurst, N, Davis, H and Burns, C (2003), 'Development of a Home Visiting Service', *Child Abuse Review* 12(3): 172-189

Boswell, G and Worthington, M (1991), 'Values for Money in Probation Practice', *Justice of the Peace* 155(51): 814-815

Bracken, D (2003), 'Skills and Knowledge for Contemporary Probation Practice', in *Probation Journal* 50(2): 101-114

Brorson, K (2005), 'The Culture of a Home Visit in Early Interventions', *Journal or Early Childhood Research* 3(1): 51-76

Buchanan, J and Millar, M (1997), 'Probation: Reclaiming a Social Work Identity', *Probation Journal* 44(1): 32-36

Burnett, R and McNeil, F (2005), 'The Place of the Officer-Offender Relationship in Assisting Offenders to Desist from Crime', *Probation Journal* 52(3): 221-242

Capps, D (1982), *Biblical Approaches to Pastoral Counselling,* Philadelphia: The Westminster Press

Carr, W (2002) (ed), *The New Dictionary of Pastoral Studies,* London: SKPC

Ciliska, D, Mastrilli, P, Ploeg, J, Hayward, S, Brunton, G and Underwood, J (2001), 'The Effectiveness of Home Visiting as a Delivery Strategy for Public Health Nursing Interventions to Clients in the Prenatal and Postnatal Period: A Systematic Review', *Primary Health Care Research and Development* 2(1): 41-54

Crosbie, A, Lowie, A and Mennie, M (1994), 'Genetic Disorders' in Alexander, M, Fawcett, J and Runciman, P (ed's), *Nursing Practice – Hospital and Home – The Adult,* London: Churchill Livingstone

D'Angelo, A (1999), 'Effectively Managing the Elderly Client in the Community', in Zang, S and Allender, J (ed's), *Home Care of the Elderly,* Philadelphia: Lippincott

Davies, K (2006), 'Case Management and Think First Completion', *Probation Journal* 53(3): 213-229

Frankel, J and Hobart, C (1998), *A – Z of Childcare – The Complete Study Guide and Project Planner,* Cheltenham: Stanley Thornes (Publishers) Ltd

Gardner, R (2005), *Supporting Families – Child Protection in the Community,* Chichester: John Wiley and Sons Ltd

Griffith-Thomas, W H (1995), *Ministerial Life and Work,* Grand Rapids: Baker Book House

Hedderman, C and Hearnden, I (2001), 'To Discipline or Punish? Enforcement under National Standards 2000', *Vista* 6(3): 215-224

Hockling, M (1985), *A Handbook of Pastoral Work – Revised Edition,* Oxford: Mowbray

Home Office (2005), *National Standards 2005,* London: Crown Copyright

Home Office (2006), *Talking Shop – Home Visits: The Key to Reducing Drug-Related Crime,* www.drugs.gov.uk/talking-shop/casestudies/homevisits?version=1

Hopkins, G (2003), 'Charity Starts at Home', *Community Care* 11-17th December 2003

Hornsby-Smith, M (1989), *The Changing Parish – A Study of Parishes, Priests and Parishioners after Vatican II,* London: Routledge

Hudson, B (2001), 'Human Rights, Public Safety and the Probation Service: Defending Justice in the Risk Society', *The Howard Journal* 40(2): 103-113

Lewis, S (2005), 'Rehabilitation: Headline or Footnote in the new Penal Policy', *Probation Journal* 52(2): 119-135

Mair, G (1997), 'Community Penalties and the Probation Service', in Maguire, M, Morgan, R and Reiner, R (ed's), *The Oxford Handbook of Criminology (2nd Edition),* Oxford: Oxford University Press

McCulloch, T and Kelly, L (2007), 'Working with Sex Offenders in Context: Which way Forward?, *Probation Journal* 54(1): 7-21

McMurray, A (1990), *Community Health Nursing – Primary Health Care in Practice,* London: Churchill Livingstone

McNaughton, D (2000), 'A Synthesis of Qualitative Home Visiting Research', *Public Health Nursing* 17(6): 405-414

McNeill, F (2004), 'Supporting Desistance in Probation Practice: A Response to Maruna, Porter and Carvalho', *Probation Journal* 51(3): 241-247

McNeill, F (2006), 'A Desistance Paradigm for Offender Management', *Criminology and Criminal Justice* 6(1): 39-62

Merrington, S (2006), 'Is More Better? The Value and Potential of Intensive Community Supervision', *Probation Journal* 53(4): 347-360

Millar, M and Buchanan, J (1995), 'Probation: A Crisis of Identity and Purpose', *Probation Journal* 42(4):195-198

National Offender Management Service (2006), *The NOMS Offender Management Model,* London: Home Office

New York City Department of Probation (2006), *Supervision,* June 2006, www.nyc.gov/html/prob/html/units_family.html

O'Connor, S and Gibson, B (2003), 'Insight into Rehabilitation', in Grandis, S, Long, G, Glasper, A and

Jackson, P, *Foundation Studies for Nursing,* Basingstoke: Palgrave MacMillan

Rex, S (1999), 'Desistance from Offending: Experiences of Probation', *The Howard Journal* 38(4): 366-383

Robertson, C (1991), *Health Visiting in Practice (2nd Edition),* London: Churchill Livingstone

Ross, A (2003), *Counselling Skills for Church and Faith Community Workers,* Maidenhead: Open University Press

Senior, P (1987), 'The Future of Probation', *Criminal Justice* August 1987: 8-9

Sturkie, K (1984), 'Adolescent Abusing Families: A Cognitive-Family Approach to Practice', in Goldstein, H, Hilbert, H and Hilbert, J (ed's), *Creative Change – A Cognitive Humanistic Approach to Social Work Practice,* London: Tavistock Publications Ltd

Vaughn, S (1984), 'The Rural Poor: Toward Self-Reliance in the Context of Family Community and Culture', in Goldstein, H, Hilbert, H and Hilbert, J (ed's), *Creative Change – A Cognitive Humanistic Approach to Social Work Practice,* London: Tavistock Publications Ltd

Worrall, A (1997), *Punishment in the Community – The Future of Criminal Justice,* Harlow: Longman

Wright, F (1982), *Pastoral Care for Lay People,* London: SCM Press Ltd

Wright, F (1996), *Pastoral Care Revisited,* London: SCM Press

About Metanoeo

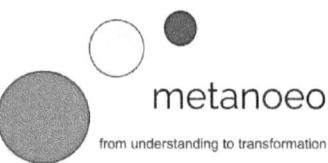

Metanoeo is a social enterprise engaging faith in the journey from crime in practice, the community and academia. In addition to training, Metanoeo offers consultancy and research services and academic courses and programmes. Metanoeo offers those at risk of addiction, antisocial and offending behaviour the opportunity to engage in a life coaching scheme to help them use their faith or openness to faith build a positive identity and lifestyle supporting the journey away from crime.

About the author

Dave has over twelve years experience as a probation practitioner and manager helping to rehabilitate those convicted of crime. He has also lectured and published in criminal and community justice and is presently completing his PhD in Theology and Criminology. Dave established Metanoeo in 2014.